...le Prospects:
...LITY
...OWN
...*shire Landscape*

Karen Lynch

With the compliments

of

Yorkshire Gardens Trust

www.yorkshiregardenstrust.org.uk

Mercer Art Gallery, Harrogate

This book celebrates the tercentenary of the birth of Lancelot 'Capability' Brown and the twentieth anniversary of the Yorkshire Gardens Trust.

It is dedicated to the memory of Philippa Rakusen (1922-2006), founder member and benefactor of the Yorkshire Gardens Trust, renowned horticulturalist and friend.

The development of a new natural style of laying out parks in the eighteenth century is acknowledged to be one of the greatest artistic achievements in British history. One man's name is indelibly linked with the profession of landscape gardening: Lancelot Brown. Achieving great renown in his own lifetime he became universally known by his affectionate nickname 'Capability', and whilst fashions in design have come and gone, his fame remains great three hundred years after his birth.

Lancelot Brown was born in the hamlet of Kirkharle, around 20 miles north west of Newcastle in rural Northumberland. His exact birthdate is not known, but he was baptised in the parish church of St Wilfrid's on 30 August 1716 as the son of William Browne. His mother's name is not given in the register and for much of Brown's early life there is little recorded history.

Sarah Davison (b..1996).
St Wilfrid's, Kirkharle, 2015.
© Sarah Davison.

LAUNCELOT BROWN Esq:
of Fenstanton Hunts.
"Capability Brown"
B.1716.   D.1783.

In 1827 the Northumberland historian John Hodgson wrote about Brown, by now Kirkharle's most famous son, and he recounted that Brown attended the local school before taking an apprenticeship in the gardens of Kirkharle Hall, the seat of Sir William Lorraine. The Brown family had close links with the Lorraines; Brown's father worked on the estate and his brother John would later marry Sir William's daughter, Jane.

In around 1739 Brown left his native Northumberland and probably moved to Lincolnshire to work on water management in the Fens, possibly with his brother John who was a surveyor. It was probably whilst in Lincolnshire that he met a local girl, Bridget Wayet, and began a courtship that would lead to marriage in 1744.

The wedding took place at Stowe, in Buckinghamshire, where Brown had found employment a few years earlier in the famous gardens of Lord Cobham. During his time at Stowe Brown worked with the most admired landscape gardener of the age, William Kent, adding Kent's artistic influence to the practical skills he had already acquired. He progressed to the role of Head Gardener and Lord Cobham also 'loaned' his prodigy to friends who wished to remodel their parks. By the time Brown left Stowe in 1751 he had an impressive curriculum vitae having worked on parks such as Wotton, also in Buckinghamshire, and Newnham Paddox in Warwickshire.

At around the same date, Brown was introduced to the Earl of Coventry, of Croome in Worcestershire. At Croome Brown designed the exterior of a new church and remodelled the mansion, and worked on the park for more than a decade. In his early days at Croome he acquired the nickname that would stay with him for life. He had a habit of telling his clients that their estate had 'capabilities', that is, potential for improvement. So frequent was his use of the phrase that he became known as Capability Brown. When his friend David Garrick, the famous actor and writer, added a joke on the subject to his popular play *Lethe* in 1757 the name became fixed in the public consciousness and the affable Brown no doubt enjoyed the gentle teasing.

the Capabilities of this Place

The Yorkshire clients that can be firmly associated with Brown were unsurprisingly drawn from the wealthy elite. Four were peers from ancient established families: the Earl of Holderness of Hornby Castle, the Earl of Scarbrough of Sandbeck, Viscount Irwin of Temple Newsam, and Baron Stourton of Stapleton. Holderness holds the distinction of having employed Brown at four estates: his country seat Sion Hill, on the edge of London, Shillington in Bedfordshire, and his two Yorkshire estates of Hornby, near Bedale, and Aston, near Sheffield. Baronets and the established gentry make up the bulk of Brown's client list with two examples of extremely wealthy men who had prospered in trade: Sir Lawrence Dundas of Aske and Edwin Lascelles of Harewood.

(left)
'The Capabilities of this Place',
from a letter from Richard Beaumont
of Whitley Beaumont to Walter Spencer
Stanhope of Cannon Hall, 1779,
Sp/St60564/161.
Courtesy of Barnsley Archives.

(right)
George Knapton (1698-1778).
The Earl of Holderness, c.1752.
Oil on canvas, 119 x 137 cm.
© Leeds Museums & Galleries
(Temple Newsam House) /
Bridgeman Images.

B Brown seems to have had little leisure time, and we don't know if he was diverted from his work to see the the great Yorkshire gardens of earlier generations such as Bramham Park, Castle Howard, Studley Royal and Duncombe Park. Happily, Brown does not appear to have looked at the capabilities of these four and they remain as monuments to the taste of the earlier generation. At Bramham the layout is largely geometrical with straight drives and avenues and formal pieces of water. At Castle Howard, Studley and Duncombe the lines are becoming softer and more sinuous, the genesis of the style that developed throughout the 1700s and reached its peak with Brown.

Early views of estates where Brown worked, including Howsham, Temple Newsam and Sandbeck, show formal gardens with regular parterres, terraces and ponds, and straight walks and drives.

John Booth (fl. early eighteenth century). Howsham One of the Seats of the Honble Sr John Wentworth Bart, 1718. Ink and wash on parchment, 75.5 x 65 cm. North Yorkshire County Record Office ZCG M 1/6.

HOWSHAM One of

T

The new natural style saw this largely swept away. Instead, expanses of lawn were planted right up to the house, and ha-has (deep ditches impassable to animals) were constructed so that the eye was tricked into seeing an unbroken stretch of green from the house to the horizon. Stock could graze beyond the ha-ha, bringing life to the scene, but could not stray onto the fine lawns close to the house. Drives were curved around contours, often allowing glimpses of the mansion or of features such as temples, and ensuring that the visitor was in no doubt as to the magnificence of the estate.

Simon Warner (b. 1951).
Ha-ha at Sledmere, 2015.
© Simon Warner.

Lakes or serpentine rivers were created by Brown to add interest to the middle ground when viewed from the house. Often the ends would be concealed with planting, keeping the illusion of a river running through, or with a sham bridge like the elegant Palladian Bridge at Scampston. Those owners lucky enough to have a genuine river would see it manipulated for aesthetic effect. New plantations encircled the estate, giving privacy and also shelter to the rides that wound through them, but were also cut through occasionally to allow the passer-by to admire the landscape within.

Simon Warner (b.1951).
Ride at Whitley Beaumont, 2015.
© Simon Warner.

View of ASK, near Richmond Yorkshire, the seat of Sᵗ THOMAS DUNDAS. Barᵗ

Janʸ 1.1792, Published by Taylor, Holborn, London.

Anonymous. View of Ask [sic],
near Richmond Yorkshire, 1792.
Engraving on paper, 9.8 x 14.8cm.
The Georgian Group Pardoe Collection.

Clumps (clusters of trees) of native trees such as oak, beech and sweet chestnut broke the expanses of lawn and meadow, and there were individual specimens of exotic newly-imported species such as Cedars of Lebanon and various firs. Meandering gravel paths, often edged with shrubs to hide them from the windows of the house, allowed the ladies to keep their feet dry when they walked out in damp weather.

The improvements were not solely to beautify the scene and display the owner's taste and wealth. An estate had to be productive as well as polished and Brown was an expert on water management, creating well-drained land for animals and crops. Brown's clients were keen to test the latest advances in husbandry and agriculture. At Sledmere, Harewood, Hornby and Aston new farmhouses were built, in a very handsome manner, to function as eye-catchers in the landscape as well as being working farms. At Hornby and Aston Lord Holderness would take guests for a drive in the carriage after dinner to admire these new buildings and their landscape setting.

Simon Warner (b. 1951).
Arbour Hill Farm, Hornby Castle,
2015. © Simon Warner.

Each landscape was also designed for the fashionable leisure pursuits of the day. Menageries, such as the one Brown planned for Temple Newsam, were usually home to exotic birds such as colourful pheasants and peacocks and had a room where the ladies could take tea after feeding the fowl. Lakes were used for fishing, bathing and boating with attendant buildings; at Hornby Brown probably suggested the site for the (now lost) thatched Fishing Temple where silk cushions enabled a comfortable wait for a bite. Eye-catcher temples doubled as banqueting or picnic houses, such as the gothic tea-house at Howsham located on one of Brown's new rides cut through the woodland. Equipped with china cups and glasses for lemonade it was also an observatory with a 'large Tellescope'.

J.C. Nattes (c.1765-1839).
S.W. View of a Castle in Howsham, 1807.
Pencil, ink and wash on paper,
24.3 x 37.8 cm.
Courtesy of Manchester City Art Gallery

S.W. View of a Castle in Howsham
Wood Sept 1807

B

Brown was not the only improver working in this style, although he was by far the most successful and famed. In Yorkshire in the same period Richard Woods, Thomas White and the Adam Mickles (father and son) were very active. White and the Mickles both worked as foremen for Brown early in their careers before establishing independent practices and White was later in competition with Brown at Harewood and Sledmere. In fact, the landscape at Sledmere became an amalgam of the two men's ideas. Christopher Sykes sought advice in 1777-78 from the 'Great Brown', as he referred to him in his diary, but the final layout mixed in some of White's ideas, as well as some of Sykes's own.

There were also lesser-known designers, their names lost to us today, and many estate owners thought themselves perfectly competent to design their own landscape. At Bretton Hall (now home to the Yorkshire Sculpture Park), Sir Thomas Wentworth had employed a professional, Richard Woods, and had not been impressed. When he embarked on further works he declared it would be without the help of 'Capability or any such pretending Rogues'

'The Great Brown', entry in the diary of Christopher Sykes of Sledmere, 1777. Hull History Centre U DDSY5/43/1, used with the kind permission of Sir Tatton Sykes.

20

Simon Warner (b.1951).
Sledmere House, 2015.
© Simon Warner.

T

This mix of improvers working in a similar style, and often in conjunction with each other, is one of the factors that makes attributing a landscape to Brown very difficult. The fourteen sites discussed in this book are all documented as being by Brown but there are others in the county that are anecdotally associated with him or have a brief reference in an early history (see summary p. 68). One such example is Wentworth Castle, which a single early source suggests is by Brown. A contemporary view by Thomas Bardwell shows it to have all the ingredients of a Brown landscape; but without evidence it remains 'Brownian' rather than Brown.

Thomas Bardwell (1704-1767),
Wentworth Castle, c.1751-2.
Oil on canvas, 119.5 x 180.5 cm.
Wentworth Castle Heritage Trust,
gifted by Charles Wentworth 2016.

Brown's usual working pattern began with a visit to a site to assess the capabilities. This would involve riding and walking around the estate with the owner. He was known to have a quick eye and he was described soon after his death as being able to assess a park in an hour. Whilst this may be an exaggeration he could certainly reach a decision very quickly: he spent two days at Aske in 1769 and only one day at Sledmere in 1777. The estate steward would have ridden alongside, for he was responsible for keeping a close eye on the improvements and the budget when the master was not at home. As largely verbal exchanges, we have little record of the discussions and decisions made along the route except at Burton Constable, in the East Riding. Here the steward, John Raines, kept detailed memoranda that he transcribed after each of Brown's visits. Such a comprehensive account of the improvements is unique in Yorkshire, and very rare across Brown's entire oeuvre.

Simon Warner (b. 1951).
Burton Constable Hall
from across the Lake, 2015.
© Simon Warner

B Brown's key tool was an accurate survey of the estate and he had his own men who would survey the topography, using the latest theodolite technology to assess the levels, and then draw up a detailed plan. Alternatively, a landowner might commission a survey from a local expert. At Aske, Hornby and Aston the Richmond-based surveyor George Jackson produced the maps and at Sledmere it was Robert Dunn. Both men had been involved with the enclosure movement, when comprehensive plans were needed for the allocation of land. At Whitley Beaumont the surveyor William Crossley was employed. He had produced designs for improvements at nearby Kirklees Park, but he would later move into the lucrative field of surveying for the rapidly expanding canal network.

J.T. Taite (fl. 1850s), Whitley Beaumont, 1858. Oil on canvas, 27 x 40cm. Courtesy of Stephen Beaumont.

W

With the survey complete Brown would present his ideas to the client, usually in the form of a large plan of what he called the 'alterations'. Although Brown is known to have been consulted at fourteen sites in Yorkshire, very few plans or documents are known to survive. The large-scale plan for Temple Newsam (1762) survives as does the plan for Sledmere (1778) although it is in a very poor condition. A smaller design for Burton Constable is attributed to Brown but is unsigned and undated. Improvements sketched onto an earlier plan of Scampston may also be in Brown's hand, but the designs for all the other estates are lost or destroyed.

Lancelot Brown (1716-1783).
A Plan for the intended Alterations at Temple Newsam, 1762.
Pen, ink and wash on paper, 180 x 140 cm. WYL 100/EA20/5A.
By arrangement with West Yorkshire Archive Service.

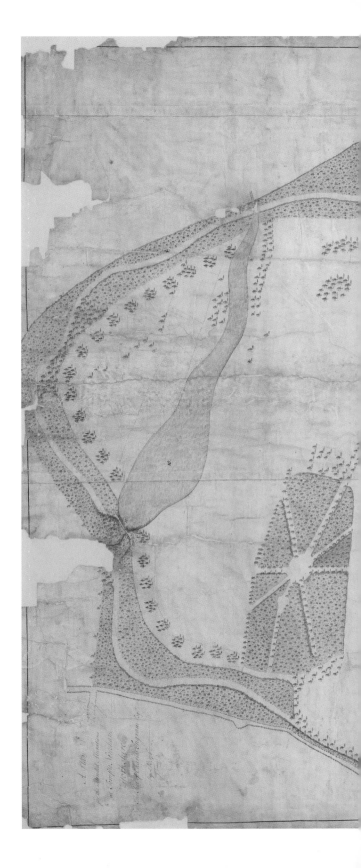

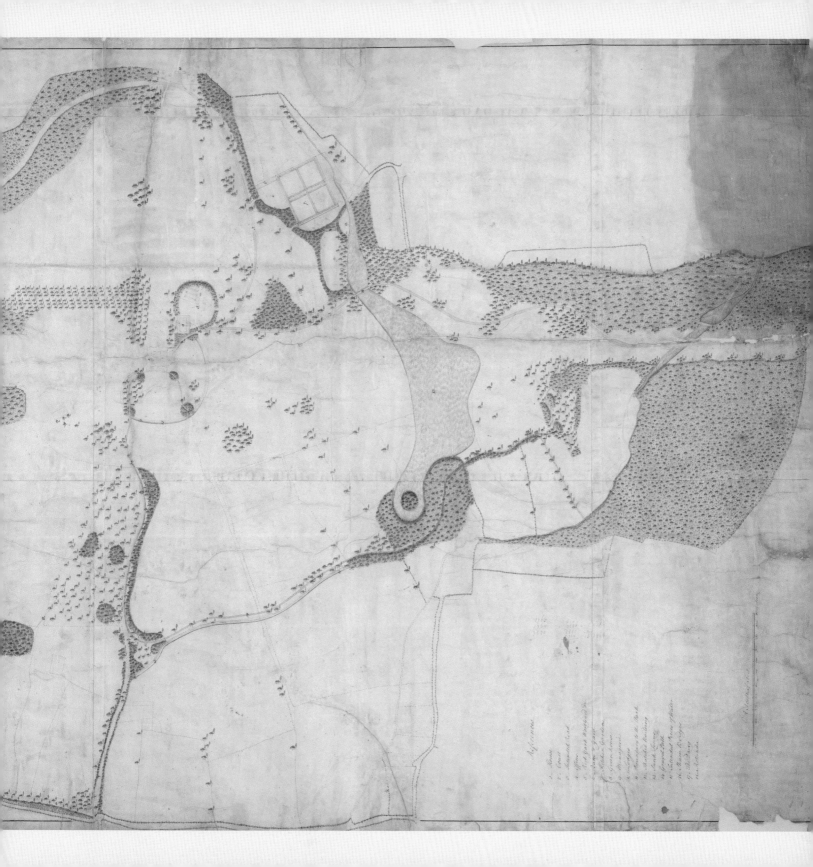

Brown may also have been involved in commissioning artists to provide views of parks as they would look following improvement. At Burton Constable a view by George Barrett of 1777 shows the lake with mature planting although accounts record that work digging out the water was still ongoing at that date. A painting of Temple Newsam attributed to Michael Angelo Rooker shows a view to the mansion across a fine lake in the form of a serpentine river. The work is not dated, but may have been painted in the early 1760s to illustrate how Brown envisaged the park would look after his improvements. Brown's plan shows a piece of water in the same location as the painting, but it was never constructed.

George Barrett (c.1732-1784).
Burton Constable seen from across
the Lake, 1777. Oil on canvas,
119.5 x 167.5cm.
Burton Constable Foundation.

Michael Angelo Rooker (1746-1801)
(attributed).
Temple Newsam.
Oil on canvas, 101 x 132 cm.
Courtesy of the Earl of Halifax.

Once the plan was received the landowner could then choose to make a contract with Brown for the implementation of the plans, or hand the work to a trusted estate employee. In Yorkshire Brown was awarded the contract to project-manage the works at Harewood, Temple Newsam and Sandbeck, but the only written contract known to survive is for the latter. Brown would appoint a foreman who would stay on site and recruit and supervise the workforce. As the business continued to expand, keeping tabs on projects and the foremen became a concern for Brown who worried that while he was 'galloping in one part of the world' his men were making 'blunders and neglects' elsewhere.

Should the client decide to use his own workforce then Brown's involvement would end when his bill was paid - usually a standard fee of 50 guineas. There are occasions when Brown seems to have revisited a site even when he was not managing the works, perhaps out of curiosity or courtesy as many clients became friends.

Simon Warner (b.1951).
The Grey Stone and Harewood House,
2015. © Simon Warner.

Often there were opportunities for Brown to submit designs for buildings as well as the landscape. At Harewood in 1758, Edwin Lascelles, probably Brown's first Yorkshire client, was finalising his decision on the site for a new house and considering plans by John Carr of York and Sir William Chambers. Brown submitted two drawings for the mansion but lost the commission to Carr. His plans for a new front at Temple Newsam were also never implemented. Scampston, as it looked at the end of the eighteenth century, would have been the only house in Yorkshire designed by Brown, but his remodelling was short-lived and the next generation destroyed his work when the house was again given a new front.

Francis Nicholson (1753-1844).
Scampston Hall, c.1790.
Watercolour and bodycolour
on paper, 30.8 x 38.2 cm.
© Chapter of York, S/7/1:
Reproduced by kind permission.

NB The Red Colour is the Office at Present
The India Ink colour the proposed Addition.

A Plan & Elevation Mr B seen rec

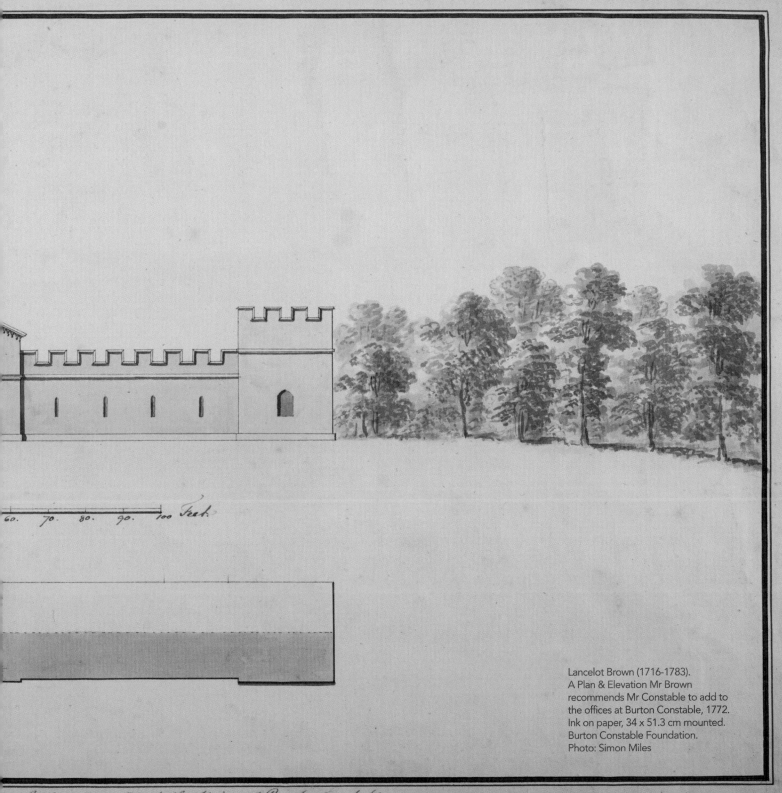

60. 70. 80. 90. 100 Feet.

Lancelot Brown (1716-1783).
A Plan & Elevation Mr Brown
recommends Mr Constable to add to
the offices at Burton Constable, 1772.
Ink on paper, 34 x 51.3 cm mounted.
Burton Constable Foundation.
Photo: Simon Miles

o Mr Constable, to add to the Offices at Burton Constable

Elsewhere in Yorkshire Brown's architectural plans were accepted. At Burton Constable he designed a new range of domestic offices in the gothic style and an elegant bridge across the lake. This utilised one of his favourite conceits of concealing a change of levels between two pieces of water with a bridge that was actually a dam. The Bowling Green Bridge at Hornby Castle performs a similar function and two sham bridges are shown on the plan for Temple Newsam, although like the lakes they were never constructed. As well as modernising the house at Scampston Brown also designed the Palladian Bridge, the solid back of which conceals the abrupt ending of the 'river', actually a lake, just behind the structure.

Simon Warner (b. 1951).
Palladian Bridge and Lake,
Scampston, 2015.
© Simon Warner.

The Malpas Gate triumphal arch at Sandbeck Park is also thought to have been designed by Brown as the dramatic entry to a sinuous new drive which curved past new lakes and plantations to reach the mansion. This was the first phase of Brown's work at Sandbeck for the Earl of Scarbrough [sic] in the 1760s.

Once this was complete the Earl turned his attention to the three valleys that converged on the overgrown ruins of the Cistercian Roche Abbey, a few miles from the hall.

(above)
Simon Warner (b.1951).
The Malpas Gate, Sandbeck Park, 2016. © Simon Warner.

(right)
Paul Sandby (1725-1809).
Roche Abbey, Yorkshire, 1768.
Watercolour and body colour on paper, 38 x 49 cm.
Museums Sheffield.

H

Here Brown created a romantic landscape of lakes and cascades by damming the stream, and made a feature of the rocky escarpment on one side of the valley. He cleared some monastic masonry to create a more picturesque scene and set the ruins within close-cropped lawns, burying the foundations. He laid out a series of walks and rides in Kings Wood with peeps through the trees down to the abbey below, and a long vista to the graceful spire of Laughton-en-le-Morthern church. Paintings of Roche from the early 1760s show a wild landscape but two decades later, after Brown's alterations, the scene is tamed and bustling with elegant tourists. Brown was criticised by some for making the site too neat and perfect, but it became a 'must-see' for tourists and was widely visited and admired.

Samuel Hieronymus Grimm
(1733-1794). Roche Abbey,
in the Grounds of Sandbeck Park,
Near Rotherham, Yorkshire, 1780.
Pen and Indian ink, watercolour
on paper, 36.2 x 52.6 cm.
Museums Sheffield.

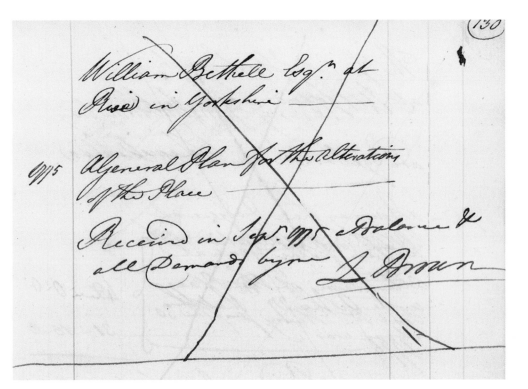

Although Brown was running a huge business, only one account book from his office is known to survive. It is a hugely important resource for learning more about Brown but also a frustrating document as it is far from comprehensive. It provides us with the sole evidence that Brown was commissioned to draw up a plan for William Bethell of Rise Park in the East Riding in 1775 as no contemporary accounts, diaries or illustrations have been found. A road was moved to enlarge the park in the same year, suggesting that improvements were underway, but no more is known.

The account book is also our main source of information on three other parks: Howsham, Byram and Stapleton. The entry for Howsham states that Brown made a plan for Nathaniel Cholmley and although undated it is listed alongside other projects in the 1770s. There are good maps and plans for Howsham in the family archive but very little in the way of correspondence or accounts. It is likely that Brown was responsible for the removal of all traces of the earlier formal garden west of the house and for replacing it with extensive lawns that swept from the mansion to a new plantation, Howsham Wood. The wood was cut through with walks and rides and the gothic teahouse provided shelter and refreshments. The new curving drive from Howsham Bridge was probably also designed by Brown and he may have suggested the embellishments to the mill, attributed to Carr, on the river Derwent that forms an eye-catcher from this drive.

Lancelot Brown's surviving account book, entry for Rise Park, 1775. Courtesy of Mr M. Morrice/Royal Horticultural Society, Lindley Library.

Simon Warner (b.1951).
Howsham Hall, 2015.
© Simon Warner.

There is firm evidence that the Earl of Holderness employed Brown at four sites, even though curiously no entries were made in Brown's account book. The Earl had been the British Ambassador Extraordinary in Venice in 1744-46 and on his return to Britain became a prominent member of the Society of Dilettanti, the salon whose membership was only open to cultured men who had travelled in Italy (although the prolific letter-writer and social commentator Horace Walpole believed it was simply an upmarket drinking den). Holderness first employed Brown in Yorkshire at his seat outside Sheffield, Aston Hall. In the early 1760s the old mansion was demolished and a new one built to the designs of John Carr. Work on the landscape was concurrent with the building of the house, and the formal gardens were replaced with a lawn that swept up to the house with a ha-ha to keep stock out of the pleasure grounds without interrupting the views over what was then open countryside (now industry and motorways). Fish ponds were adapted to create lakes and clumps and plantations used to define and embellish the parkland.

J. McGahey (fl. first half nineteenth century). Aston Hall, undated. Watercolour and bodycolour on paper. Courtesy of Rodney & Peter Varelst, photo: Warren Bellette.

J ohn Carr was also employed at Hornby a few years later, but this time to remodel the ancient castle. Whilst Carr modernised the house, Brown was at work on the landscape, creating a grass terrace around the castle that then rolled gently down to a string of serpentine lakes that appeared as a river from the higher ground by the mansion. A rustic bridge masked the change of levels of two of the slim lakes that made up the 'river' and formed a scene with the Bowling Green House, a gothic banqueting house of 1760. Huge amounts of earth were moved to create the gentle banks and ha-has were dug out. Also visible from the terrace as eye-catchers were some of the ornamental farms whose positions were probably decided by Holderness in consultation with Brown. New rides created a circuit for excursions in the carriage to admire the park. Holderness's chaplain, Revd William Mason, was his advisor on matters aesthetic as well as spiritual, and appears to have been involved with the improvements at Hornby and Aston, where he had a rectory with its own designed landscape.

J. Miller (fl. 1840s). Hornby Castle,
Yorkshire, 1847.
Oil on canvas, 43.5 x 61.1 cm.
Private Collection/Photo
© Christie's Images/Bridgeman Images.

H

Holderness was also briefly the owner of Aske Hall, near Richmond, which he inherited from his uncle in 1758. Hornby was only a few miles away down the Great North Road (the modern A1M) so Aske was sold in 1762 to Sir Lawrence Dundas, known as the Nabob of the North because of the immense wealth he had accumulated supplying the army. Brown visited in 1769 and again in 1770 and although there was a flurry of activity in the next few years, not enough records survive to be sure exactly what was executed to his plans. Brown's account book records a design for a bridge, possibly the classical bridge that survives on the Richmond to Gilling road that is shown in a painting by the Richmond artist George Cuit the elder. This painting may be another example of an artwork created to show how the park would look after improvements. Cuit was paid 15 guineas by Dundas in 1769, just as Brown was making his first proposals, and possibly this was payment for this view and its pair.

George Cuit (1743-1818).
Aske Hall, view from the south,
c. 1769-1780. Oil on canvas,
82cm x 108 cm.
Courtesy of the Zetland Collection.
Photo: Simon Miles.

Viscount and Viscountess Irwin of Temple Newsam had been keen to commission Brown since 1760 but it was 1762 before they could get him to provide a plan and another three years before work began. In that year, 1765, the Irwins added a pastoral landscape by Claude Lorraine to their art collection. Claude was immensely popular in England at this date, as were his contemporaries Poussin and Salvator Rosa and their works were found in practically every mansion Brown visited in Yorkshire. The Claudean landscapes composed of rocks, woods, water and classical architecture greatly influenced Brown and his clients.

At Temple Newsam the Claude did more than inspire the new arcadian park, it also provided respite for Lady Irwin when all outside was mud and in what she called a 'woful dirty pickle'. In the winter of 1766-67 she wrote to a friend to say that to ignore the cold and mess she would gaze upon her 'beauteous Claude where the scene always enchants me, the trees are green, the water placid and serene & the air has a warmth very comfortable'.

Claude Lorrain (1604-5?-1682).
Pastoral Landscape, mid-seventeenth century.
Oil on canvas, 94.5 x 117 cm.
Courtesy of the Earl of Halifax.

Lady Irwin didn't have to wait too long for her own version of paradise for by 1767 the improvements were greatly admired. In that year an anonymous poem was published celebrating Brown's work and dedicated to Lord Irwin. *The Rise and Progress of the Present Taste in Planting Parks, Pleasure Grounds, Gardens…* praises Brown's work across the country before eulogising Temple Newsam in a section that includes the following lines:

Delighted still along the Park we rove,
Vary'd with Hill and Dale, with Wood and Grove:
O'er velvet Lawns what noble Prospects rise
Fair as the Scenes, that Reuben's hand supplies!

The poem goes on to mention a proposed lake, but although two pieces of water are shown on Brown's plan neither was ever constructed. Brown did construct a new drive in his favoured meandering style with sphinx-topped gates, and laid out gravel paths edged with shrubs. He also created new plantations and artfully arranged clumps of trees in the park. Some of the features on his plan may never have been built although the menagerie is remembered in a wood by that name and a small porticoed temple survives on the spot marked 'rotunda' on the plan.

Simon Warner (b.1951).
Sphinx Gate at Temple Newsam,
2015. © Simon Warner.

By the 1770s Brown's fame was widespread and he struggled to keep up with projects across England and Wales. Inevitably he had to turn work away, especially in more distant parts. A potential client in the Scottish Borders lamented that Mr Brown was not 'come-at-able' and when asked to look at an estate in Ireland Brown is said to have excused himself on the grounds that he had not 'finished England yet'.

Simon Warner (b. 1951).
Roche Abbey, 2015.
© Simon Warner.

In Yorkshire alone in that decade he continued the work at Sandbeck and had new projects at Scampston, Howsham, Rise, Sledmere and Whitley Beaumont. In 1772 he returned to Harewood to implement the plans for the lake and park that had been discussed back in 1758. Drives were created that wound in and out of the new plantations and showed the house and park to great advantage. Cascades were constructed on the Eccup Beck to be viewed on the approach to the house, and by the new Rustic Bridge cobbles were laid in the water to disturb the flow and create sound: a further sensory experience. The stylish and technologically advanced kitchen garden and home farm were also included on the circuit, demonstrating Edwin Lascelles's wealth, good taste and knowledge of horticulture, agriculture and husbandry. A massive amount of earth moving was required to sculpt the ground around the house, to dig out a series of ha-has and of course to form the lake. These improvements continued over a decade and Brown's bank account shows a total cost of £6,203.00, his most expensive commission in Yorkshire.

J.M.W. Turner (1775-1851),
Harewood House from the South, 1798.
Graphite and watercolour on paper,
45.7 x 65.2 cm.
Courtesy of the Executors of the
7th Earl of Harewood and the Trustees
of the Harewood House Trust.

Simon Warner (b. 1951),
Bridge at Burton Constable,
2015. © Simon Warner.

In 1772 Brown also returned to Burton Constable where his 1760s plans had been abandoned whilst William Constable went off on a Grand Tour of Europe. This would be another project that lasted for around a decade and the works are recorded in the detailed memoranda kept by the estate steward. There was extensive landscaping in addition to the offices, lakes and bridge mentioned earlier. Over the years the works were constantly revised to meet Brown's high standards: islands were created in the lake and then taken away again and the lake was widened, enlarged, and resculpted on a number of occasions. Some of the formal avenues were 'clumped', a typical Brown solution that enabled many mature trees to be saved rather than felled: sections of the avenue were removed and the remaining trees were formed into clumps with the addition of new planting. A hill was shaved to allow more light into the park, ha-has were dug out and gravel walks were constructed through shrubberies. William Constable summarised the work as 'levelling and uniting grounds, forming swells, laying down pieces of water, making plantations & […] beautifying & finishing a place with the most accurate neatness'.

Meticulous planning went into Brown's excursions to different parts of the country to visit his clients, so his visit to Burton Constable in 1772 would have been arranged to include a look at Scampston, just over the border into the North Riding near Malton. Following his 1772 visit, Brown sent Sir William St Quintin a plan of the estate (now lost), which we know included a ha-ha and changes to the existing pieces of water to create the 'new river', complete with island. In 1773 he sent plans for a cascade and for the Palladian Bridge and probably the designs for the remodelling of the house.

Francis Nicholson (1753-1844),
Cascade at Scampston, c.1790.
Watercolour and bodycolour on
paper, 31 x 38 cm. Courtesy of the
Legard Family of Scampston.

A

As the 1770s drew to a close Brown visited Whitley Beaumont near Huddersfield, the seat of Richard Henry Beaumont. The plan he sent in 1779 is lost but from correspondence we know it included a new carriage drive from Lepton to the south that wound through woodland and out into meadow, in marked contrast to the earlier dead-straight formal approach from the north. Work on Brown's 'ornamental designs' also included plantations cut with rides that encircled the estate, ha-has, and clumps of trees punctuating the landscape. Although the parkland was damaged by coal extraction during the Second World War, and the house demolished in the 1950s, the outline of Brown's design is still very much visible today.

Whitley Beaumont, 2015.
228824_035 ©Historic England Archive

In 1782 Brown was again at Burton Constable to see how the alterations had progressed. On that same Yorkshire excursion he also met two new clients. At Byram, near Ferrybridge, the Ramsden family papers are again sparse and although Brown's account book tells us that Brown and his surveyor made visits, and then sent a plan in December 1782, there are no accounts or plans known to survive. A letter of the following year talks of the 'profusion' of improvements underway for Sir John Ramsden 4th Bart so it is likely that Brown's design was at least partly implemented. A later generation was not so keen on the pastoral landscape, and the 'cows coming right up to the windows', so a formal terrace was built. The parkland was badly damaged by coal mining in the 1920s and the house allowed to decay until the central section collapsed. Apart from some perimeter plantations there is little of the eighteenth-century landscape to see today.

Revd Richard Hale (1773-1854).
Byrom [sic], watercolour on paper,
13.4 x 19.5 cm. Courtesy of Yorkshire
Archaeological and Historical Society and
reproduced with the permission of Special
Collections, Leeds University Library,
YAS Mackenzie 5.15.4.

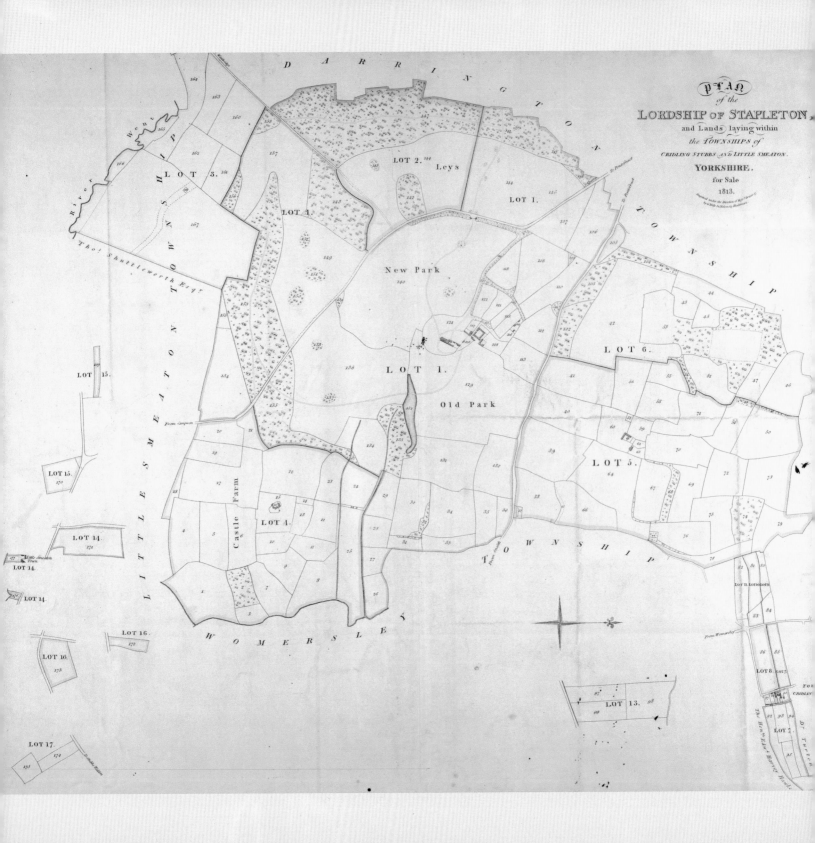

PLAN
of the
LORDSHIP OF STAPLETON,
and Lands laying within
the TOWNSHIPS of
CRIDLING STUBBS AND LITTLE SMEATON.
YORKSHIRE.
for Sale
1813.

The second new estate with capabilities was Stapleton Park, near Pontefract. Brown's account book again tells us that a surveyor attended and a plan was drawn up. Baron Stourton had only just taken occupation of Stapleton that year and the park must have been a priority but no records survive recording the works. A set of particulars produced when the estate was put on the market some twenty years later show an estate with Brown favourites such as an irregular lake, plantations around the edge of the park and scattered clumps within. The details talk of shrubberies, drives and extensive woods so it would appear that Brown influenced the layout.

En route to Yorkshire to see Stapleton and Byram in the autumn of 1782, Brown had written to the Duke of Rutland to urge him to press on with the proposed works at his Belvoir Castle estate as 'Brown grows very old'. He was in his late 60s and was not in the best of health, having suffered from asthma throughout his career. He died on 6 February 1783 and was buried in the parish church at Fenstanton, in what was then Huntingdonshire, where he was Lord of the Manor. A monument was erected to his memory with verses by his Yorkshire friend Revd William Mason. The inscription praises Brown not only as a genius in his field but also as a Christian, husband, father and friend.

(far left)
Engraved by G. Mills. Plan of the Lordship of Stapleton and lands laying within the townships of Cridling Stubbs and Little Smeaton, 1813. Engraving on paper, 65.8 x 56.5cm. The Gott Collection (Wakefield Council Permanent Art Collection).

(left)
Lancelot Brown's signature from his contract with the 4th Earl of Scarbrough, 1774. Courtesy of the Earl of Scarbrough.

Summary of Yorkshire Parks
where Capability Brown was consulted

With approximate dates of Brown's involvement.

ASKE near Richmond for Sir Lawrence Dundas, 1769-1770.

ASTON near Sheffield for the 4th Earl of Holderness, 1760s.

BURTON CONSTABLE for William Constable, 1760s, 1772-1782.

BYRAM near Ferrybridge for Sir John Ramsden, 4th Baronet, 1782.

HAREWOOD near Leeds for Edwin Lascelles, 1758, 1772-1781.

HORNBY CASTLE near Bedale for the 4th Earl of Holderness, c.1760s.

HOWSHAM near Malton for Nathaniel Cholmley, c.1770s.

RISE near Hull for William Bethell, 1775.

SANDBECK PARK AND ROCHE ABBEY near Rotherham
for the 4th Earl of Scarbrough, 1760-1779.

SCAMPSTON near Malton for Sir William St Quintin 5th Baronet, 1772-73.

SLEDMERE near Driffield for Christopher Sykes, 1777-78.

STAPLETON near Pontefract for the 17th Lord Stourton, 1782.

TEMPLE NEWSAM near Leeds for the 9th Viscount Irwin, 1762-1771.

WHITLEY BEAUMONT near Huddersfield for Richard Henry Beaumont, 1779-80.

The following sites have traditionally been associated with Brown but research has found no evidence to confirm he was consulted: Birdsall House, Cannon Hall, Goldsborough Hall, Hollin Hall, Ripley Castle, Sutton Park, Wentworth Castle and Woodsome Hall.

Further Reading

Jane Brown *The Omnipotent Magician: Lancelot 'Capability' Brown* 1716-1783
(London: Chatto & Windus, 2011)

Karen Lynch, 'Capability Brown in Yorkshire', *Yorkshire Capabilities: New Arcadian Journal 75/76* (2016), pp. 37-107. (An extended and fully referenced version of the present text).

Dorothy Stroud *Capability Brown* (London: Faber & Faber, 1975)

Simon Warner (b.1951).
The Lake at Harewood, 2015.
© Simon Warner.

For over 160 years we have provided advice to our clients, working to solve their problems, take advantage of opportunities and turn advice into action.

For more information, please contact Alison Robinson on T: +44 (0)1423 568012 or E: alison.robinson@saffery.com.

Alternatively, visit www.saffery.com.

Saffery Champness
CHARTERED ACCOUNTANTS

Savills, making a difference delivering bespoke property advice from town to country.

The UK's leading multi-sector property advisor

Estate Management ♦ Food & Farming ♦ Commercial Heritage
Forestry ♦ Energy ♦ Minerals ♦ Architecture and Building Surveying
Sporting ♦ Planning ♦ Valuation ♦ Farm & Residential Agency
Development ♦ Commercial ♦ Leisure ♦ Mapping ♦ International

For more information please contact Elizabeth Nelson on
01904 617836 or your local Yorkshire office

Savills York
14 Merchantgate
York YO1 9TU
01904 617800
savills.co.uk

Savills Leeds
City Point, 29 King Street
Leeds LS1 2HL
0113 244 0100

savills

Acknowledgements

This book could not have been written without the assistance of the librarians and archivists who enabled my research; the kind support of the public, private and institutional custodians of Brown landscapes in Yorkshire; and the generosity of all the owners of the artworks featured within.

Above all I would like to thank my wonderful family and friends for their love and support whilst I worked on this project.

The Yorkshire Gardens Trust would like to thank the following for their support:

Savills, The Landscape Agency, Saffery Champness and Coutts; Arnold Burton Charitable Trust; ArtFund (through a Jonathan Ruffer Curatorial Research Grant); The Calmcott Trust; The Capability Brown Festival 2016 funded by the Heritage Lottery Fund; The Friends of the Mercer Art Gallery; Harrogate Borough Council and the Mercer Art Gallery; Historic Houses Association Yorkshire Friends; Leeds Philosophical and Literary Society; Natural England; Mr & Mrs J. Samuel.

Every effort has been made to acknowledge sources and to obtain requisite consent to reproduce material.

Book design and print production by Neville Barker Design.
neville.barker@btconnect.com

Printed and bound by tig.
www.tig.uk.net

Published by Harrogate Borough Council and the Yorkshire Gardens Trust

Text copyright Karen Lynch, 2016

ISBN: 978-1-898408-21-5